What the Cracks Speak

Other Books by Steven Helmicki:

The Ballerina with Brass Knuckles in Her Purse

Remedy Lane

Healing Hands of Women

The Seduction of Loneliness

Philosophical Sayings from the Eccentric Orbit

What the Cracks Speak
Steven Christopher Helmicki

To the close friends I have been fortunate to have known. To those I have been able to help. To those who have challenged my manhood in such a way as to change the course of living. To always being as tough as one can be in any situation is my ultimate dedication. Be the antidote for adversity. Make friends.

The world softly creeps

By my door

A shadow falls

Cascading a nightmare

Played in the lights reflection

On my wall

I see you spitting noises

The curtains move

A breeze reaches my nasal passage

To a dream

On a beach we passionately wrestle

For more time.

Convalescing in my thoughts
Turn to the absurd
You and me
Under a dingy blanket
Covered in the lies
Love keeps out
The speech writer
In us all
Turns a deaf ear
To the audience
Perception beyond the act
Of contrition
In sickness and in health
In good times and bad
You and me
Stuck together on an Island
Of our own expectation
That we would be fixed
By each other
We see reality.

The act of fornication
Brandished inside men
Fear the loss
Of pleasuring women
With tongues and hands
Finger and toes
The mallet
We construct
The aura of cunnilingus
And penetration
Lust and betrayal
Rage and pleasure
Appease the want
Of seeing just glimpses
Of your most appetizing parts
Trapped by my lips

Under the construction of the psyche

Is the tunnel of doubt

I will ever relive

Remember that time on Sumner Street

Three boys held me

To the way of the streets

I learned to kill fear

By numbing with rage

The happiness passes out

Of me comes hardness and

Distrust of relatives

Who always say what's best

Only for themselves.

Some moment we realize
The desire never to do bad
Again is too similar
The old days of self-fulfillment
Of an empty heart
Kept the streets lusty
And unforgiving
The cold hard facts
Of poverty close
On my empty stomach
I arose to adulthood
Looking for fill
In for dad
Was my downfall
The emptiness
That was really a hole
Too big a puncture
To stop the bleeding
Implies we feel
The same about each other
Cautious.

A reference to insecurity

Homophobia eats white boys

By the dozens

Clamor uncomfortable with themselves

They lash out

Fag for no other reason

Than themselves.

I ask a trigger point
Hollow pierces through
My exterior just overlaps
Abandonment taped by fear
Questions arise from tears
moments away from
Breakdown the game
Film plays your hatred
Over this again
Is simply your problem
Is the discomfort
The old man
Caused your rage
To go away
Will take only but you.

After shock

The bed waves

Goodbye the memory

Of asses soil sheets

Responding to net

The sexual misgivings

Of hippies and loners

Assassins and aliens

The wet gash of a princess

Who just passed through

The pleasure gates of temptation

And deliver us from evil

I grind a wet exorcism

Of hormones into belief.

Amen.

The campaign against
Silence is under rated
Well below value
The argument we do
Tend to indulge emotion
With the temptation
Of superiority comes
A cry for a crumb of recognition
All most complaining is worth.

Underscore my name
Is assigned to service
Old family debts
Of over due emotion
Corrosive but on bare skin
The bitterness burns
Dinner and beats the dog
Every night the paper
Tells us harmony
Just isn't supposed to be
Seen anywhere in a two mile radius
Of Holy Name.

The brisk pace
Of forty odd years
Condensed into a file
Of hesitation grows
The journey towards
Ideologies sunk
And surfaced as desperation
Grabbing at liquid
Gasping for air
The splashes silence
Pleas for help
Are left answered by ourselves
We live or die.

Joke giggled
In rage
Passive observance
Testy intervention
Confrontation
In the streets
The rules are different
Old west with a bit of little Italy
Pinching and popping
The territory's trade
Crimson spills of the past
A life striving for power
Deconstructed.

War and peace in my head
A nightingale fever in the night
A simple path of 10,000 dreams interpreted
Baby names and a drug handbook
Of stones and strength intellectuals
Comes poems for the millennium
The art of the renaissance
Dreams from my father
The battles
The century
The origin of species mapping the deep
A companion to English literature
Fear and loathing in Buffalo
Dusty bookshelves
Pearl's keys to the inner universe
A light dims to
Five rings, six crises, seven dwarfs
And 38 ways to win an argument
All about the trivia of ourselves.

Master hand strength

A finger at a time

Pecking thoughts

Through electricity

And light

Background emphasizes

Bold words

Emotional statements

We become sentimental

About our own art

Striving towards masterpiece.

The last fine time

We had over dinner

At Scharf's with old fashioned

Muddled whiskey and schnitzel

Carried to a jeep

From the war zone

Of a nursing home

To ashes in my library

Comfortable those last years

Head down on Frank's bar

The nightcap for Schiller Park

A wobbly walk on Peace Street

Spinning tires on Block

Different directions from one place

Hopefully heaven is for you

Loretta.

Intently stares away

From the self

Comes disdain

A boy patterned

In the camouflage

Of a smile

Artificially lit by manipulation

the currency of getting along

a canal swallows footsteps and pain

everyone asks why

when they already know

they always have.

Conceal a weapon

Loaded with memories

Misfires and empty chambers

No danger of shooting straight

At him comes babies and crime

Thousands of days of lost time

The trenches of our underbelly

Locked up, cooped up and fucked up

Going crazy to get out and living crazy

To get back in is inevitable

Bragging about surviving their

Is just too powerful

A friend.

The answers unfold
In the dirt
Squirming scrambled
Worming deeper into myself
I get to the bottom
On one breath
The liquid clearer
Only the surface soiled
With the pollution of jealousy
Some rain dilutes it away
To further shores
I can see my own reflection
For what it is
Below me I stand strong.

Cracked tree branches
In grim lighting
Bamboo grows before
A window I peer
A picture of mother
Chess pieces and a hand gripper
Captains of crush
A candle less holder
No screened view
Of a stovepipe
The window cracked
For fresh air
Is patience.

The worse lucky

Is not seeing it for ourselves

We play martyr

To inadequacy

The choicest option

To our self imposed unhappiness

God wished more

Than street corner

Bars and lonely late night

Walks on the tracks

One side danger

One side love

From up above

I am watched over

Time from great story

Tellers I come

To you this place

In time

You will understand

I am happy

To be me

Is self knowledge

That I am

Attractive.

Grotesque distortion

Echoes guitar strings

A solo show

Of Van Halen

On the east side of buffalo

Roamed into Nugent

Jerry turn the volume down

The street mothers scream

About the noise of teenage boys

Rock star sons of drunken fathers

In laws angst

Fuck the old lady

Up the street

The song plays on

In air and a sing along

From the girls

At the corner

Later we meet

Kissing in storefronts

For hours just to

See tits.

Mamma loves our
Little girl in a GI cap
The swagger warms us
All that little happiness
Somehow came from this
Somewhat misguided
Love affair
From childhood
A fire struck stare
Quickly turn away
The back and forth
That led to today.

Simple paths on Lilac Street

Dreams from a beaten old lady

Are alive on the canals of Venice

Bombs dropping while hanging laundry

Ducking in bed sheets

A child watches silently

Vowing against the disturbance

A background for human stamina

To will the mind from insanity

Grandsons hear those old bombs

Even explode

In the memories of their children

The insane suffer twice.

Sophie's hope
For Kenny was thinness
All the old Polish ladies
Would comment how fat
He got what they fed him
A life sentence to ridicule
The old Broadway Market
Polish sticks of provolone
From under skirts in buckling shoes
Waddling vinyl shopping bags
Block after block
To pudgy babies
All winterized
Year round
They jiggle at lawn fetes
Shovel for hours
Silence their husbands
Always wanting more
French provincial
And immaculate floors
Pomeranians that bite
Men need us to have
Control of the money
Is what my mother
Taught me that men
Drink it away
All that work for
stuffed cabbage and a constant
Bitching in his ear.

Sitting alone at

A three top

In shouting

Distance from the bar

Speaking sarcastically

About ignoring his wife

Split the house in half

For the duration

He exerted his Polish

Power struggle with his will

Be done all over Buffalo

This duck isn't cooked enough

suspenders venture to the side

hot coffee legs spread out

Santa's belly napkin covered

the mobster behind the bar

mother fuck's the game

how much on it

a Saturday nights' tips

remember the aerospace days

a sky blue caddie

with white trim

a tooth pick and fedora

long overcoat and a blond

in a fur all on the corner

of Niagara Stacks says

your from Polish royalty

the other guy is a dirt digger

the neon reads

dinner and drinks
the crowd rolls into
the noise of ice on glass
laughter and flirtation
an excuse me bump
to the service station
at the bar
getting my ass pinched
a double vodka rocks
lime I'll take it outside
on the winter patio
no cigarettes just the smoke
off clear booze and the air
breathe chilly drink a warming
of the stomach acid
Sheehan says you got
A deuce on fourteen
Benny's got the drinks.

Word from the Decarlo
Gallery whispers eccentricity
The value of philanthropy
In striking spaces
Echo progress
The L pendulum swings
With passion the display
Cases of feeling created
From feminine hands
Wearing art
The world needs
To see itself
From its chairs
Caress you to unguarded
Paralysis where you
See beauty in silver gold
Platinum oil paint
Enchanting blonde
The music happy
Poetry the conversation
Even the most resistant
Can't help but smile
Jewelry to reflect ourselves
Caverns of our individualism
In someone else's creativity
We contemplate all this beauty
over L-tinis
shaken not stirred.
To think
All here in East Aurora.

The simple elegance
Of peace and the quiet
Listen to one think
Thumb on the chin
A secretary to my mind
This is all one can do
Give from the inside.

Leaning elbows
On the bed
You stand stiff-legged
To be taken
On a rainy afternoon moaning
For the peace
Of an afternoon nap.

the vulgar ness of double joints
and the liberty with language
say it to you
in tones and colors
the draft carries my misuse
past your ears
trumpets frustration
a dictionary of chides
defining the lower class
what's up
you say a street corner
store loitering for inspiration
an old man shoos away
future plans
wash away in liquor
the trouble with neighborhood bars
joints you roll into one day
staying a lifetime
is they're comfortable.

Depression stains pants
Loses the quarters for the Laundromat
Behind the mattress
Lays the bills
Crumbled up money
Pizza boxes and fog
7 day old underwear
Hunger for days
Gorging creamscicles
Bellyaching to a pillow
Drooled with despair
Faded by the sun
Warms half back
To life returns the drive
To succeed in defeating
The traps of this space
Called life.

The breath of trumpets

Rumbles exhaling motivation

The pace flat

The rope slack

No resistance

The other end down

Around the corner of poverty and despair

A lucky strike

The match burns

To fantasy

A nautilus pullover

Followed by traps

And chins

My hands on

The stopwatch

Says punishment.

Trust determines
A foothold strong
Minds alike
· Confused partitions
Light and darkly painted
Rooms open and close
Around me a corner
To stand in
Facing the end of two walls
Forces a turn around
The world sees
The real me
First time appearance
Back stage passes
By blondes in school girl skirts
Churches and bars
Frequent both
The penance and the sin.

Love ends in a Donald duck
Piloted toy plane
Dead fish in the gravel
Tolstoy's War and Peace
A film canister
Weighs memories
Keys to progress
Winning sumo watching
From aron to zoe
Dreams interpreted
What will be pulled
From the cherry bookcase
Is mystery and drama
All captured
In words.

The downtown prodigy
Glides over the plan
Key notes and other bargains
An act of regression
To the dive platform
The inviting water
Actually concrete
Foolishness paralyzed
Without another try.

Cherry licorice

Grape fish

Footsteps

For penny candy

The lottery split three ways

Trades negotiated

In front of television

The sugar high begins.

What does gotham

Let us get away

American women

The bat mobile

Heads to rushford lake

Dam walls

Echo passion

Taking place on pontoons

Coasting into docks

Tied up to a bonfire

Sipping peace from

The laps of companions

Laughter stirs the water

A night cap

As the sliding glass door

Closes another summer

Filed under the old days

Remembered during sleep.

Triumphantly silent
Moments go by
The current sleeps
Benignly close
To the edge
Been overboard
Down past danger
The curse of bravery
Squandered in the slums
One moment love
Followed by death
It all seems to disappear
Time that is gone
Just yesterday we played
Together gone down
This side of the tracks
Seems safest.

A cast from a shell
Of esteem
Evaporates in chides
Of self-conscious
Utterances and occurrences
In parks and restaurants
Parking lots and beaches
The annoyance of humanity
We gather to be alone
In stride with anger
Blaming each other
For times weren't even
There you see
Was right
About you
It is still
Mystery.

The mixture swirls

Emotion

In the grind

Of truth

A monster

Is between us

The grab of stakes

In the eyes of a child

It rains

Need.

The excuse

From the table

Covered in past due

Eleventh hour paid

A visit

To the infirmed

The television preaches

Giving money

For all your time

On earth a preacher's benefits

Grow with desperation

The post office delivers

The last few bucks

And everyone before.

Someone poisoned me
With their insecurities
Residually sicken me
On a rock sits
No one
Out the window
A guitar strums
Out of tune
We gather
Hugging and laughing
Living a concert
On the floor
Risking life and limb
To dance
In self-nourishment.

The car rides alone
A river projects
Current ambitions
The sun shines a lonely mile
Adds to the odometer
A split decision
No winners
Just frustration.

The point of view
Is straight
Behind sideways
In the back of a building
We do it
To an audience of bricks
You scrap and crawl passion
Your high heels off the ground
Lifted to contentment
The hard way
YOU LIKE IT HOT.

The captivation
Of partnership
In the scope of dreams
Becoming you
Nearly unearthed me
From more than a shallow grave
The site of rescue
Marked with memories.

The crowd around me
Is a wall
Of frustrations end
May never come
Of this work greatness
Composed in bites
Conquesting emotion
Into the trap of words
I am caught preaching
To you love
The ambition is clear
An iron mind of needs
Takes me
Higher to spaces
Above desire
To a peaceful intermingled
Nap in the clouds
Gazing at ants
Dedicated to themselves.

So ask of me

Reclined on a sofa

To rub away

The pain

In your feet originate

There you are

Emotionally infirmed

Unfeeling the hours

Of kneading

You ask when

Will I begin

Over convincing you

Right here I have been.

Read the news
A few days back
A sale and murder
With pudding spilled
A re-read on the pot
All somewhat distant
Anonymous players
Act a fool
Tributes misspelled
Buffalo news
About a bank
Bait shops
Skating

The world gets conquered

From the hands of men

Deals shake and squeeze

Someone is pinch gripped

From time

It ends at knuckles

Bloody and maimed

No one will shake them

Hold them

Be embraced by them

Trust them.

Many ways
Story has been
Told of second chances
Delayed to the slumber
Of pantyhose and lemonade
A summer sale
On memories we picnic
To the delight of a nap
We awaken with both
Desire and pleasure digested
We frantically reach
For anything satisfying
Each other.

The world beats softly
On the tethers of my soul
Sanity dangles
In God's hands
The below gravity pulls
Desire and need
Our humanness exposed
In every pub, hotel room
And concert backstage
The worry prayer
Of the cast
Heard past the curtain of clouds
Insecurities ring through monologues
Stunned audiences a gasp
In the stress of reality.

No regrets

To speak of them

Foolish choices

Everyone defined by imperfection

The morning comes new

Awakening clear

We review the time

Ahead of us

Is where it matters

When it is all over.

The mingling of substance and feeling

Noticed by strangers

In an elevator

Push the different buttons

Of height doors open

And close on passive conversation

The smells of what if

We were trapped

In someone else's world

Devours me excruciatingly

Resisting to my uniqueness.

The science of song
Filters past pre-judgment
Like smoke it permeates
All of my clothes and senses
Leaving me
Emotional residue
Covers every opportunity
A dance move
Stricken to passion
Like lazy lovers
Waking by the ocean
We sweat ourselves
To sleep
As the tide creeps
Painstakingly close
To my mouth and nose
Remain un-drowned
By magical recession
The moon my angel.

What of this big necked

Mother fucker

Sawed off

Monster of rage

Brushes babies hair

Caressing compassion

In his eyes

Rub the salt of destiny

Confronting life straight on

Not ducking

The slightest bit

Of peace I seek

Sidelines not goal lines

 My words just

Real authentic hurt

The harm of

Of it always

Came down to fists.

The crop of feelings
Picked up by hand
The heart land
Barren soiled
The ghost of harvest
In my stomach pains
Your memory told me
You molested my hope
Secretly segregating it
From reality
Became slavery.

Into and out of old classrooms

Ghosts of nuns and brothers

Eraser in hand

Time washed the blackboard clean

Of lessons can be barely read

Underneath memories of selfish consumption

Of time the world owns

All of us in its tailspin

Swimming against

Godly currents

Eventual overcome

Even the most powerful hedonist

Will kneel

When threatened with eternity.

The campus hobo

Begs not for poverty

But greed in the right

To not pay

Their way owed

By us

Just because

He has grief

To spread around

The happy pockets

Of free thought.

Whatcha gonna do
When it all stops
Spinning and running
These days the keyboard
Screams passion
In the gothic fog
Of a pitch black club
Stare at the Continental mirror
Say goodbye in a grinding dance
The lights come on
Like morning after
Everyone packs up
And leaves without a goodbye.

Influence me in time

For a soulful prayer

Kneeling blocks from

Wall Street

Dirty deeds done

The tide of trade

Grips us

The money trail

Visible and near

Our emptiness seduced

By Egyptian cotton and silk

Exotic skin on shoes

Pull the finest wool

Over our conscience

Sipping single malt fate

The gamble is akin

To good versus evil

Questioned downed to the core

We stare down with temptation

And blink.

I have been down Block Street

In its' alleys and fields

Followed the tracks

To forts

Skateboarded to the drama 269

Up doat hill

The cutoff Bailey

Guides me left

To lovejoy

The nineteen bus

A backseat ride

The catholic school girls'

Sacred hearts

And bra straps snapped

Between swigs of quarts

In chess king leather jackets

Roaming for a meeting

With hope and a moving

Van took us

To some better place

Safe from our own kind.

The refinery of booze
The creative mind
Blows in fog
A tapping and pecking
Deleting emotion
Crossing out
Some of the time
This all makes
Sense of ourselves
To others we compel
Truth in the dawn
Hour spent
Trying to get your
Attention is with
Cartoons.

Boisterous writing
Clamors on walls
In light life rhythms
With vision
The telephone
Teaches us ourselves
The nature of marketing
Dreams to the penniless
For a price
America brings you
Hope you like tricks.

The compounding of thought

A complexity of our time

Teases freedom

Is all a limited perspective

A deviant of its original form

Choices made decry

In the nighttime

Relieve myself

Of the overcrowded

Desires begging for

An exit.

A view to a kill

Myself the roadside

By a small town

Closes in

The defense

Of a dog

Sprung loose

By hormones

Rubber ceased

After the metal

Consequences

Lust with death.

Jesus befriended me

A drunk ride home

Guided straight

Artificially content

The free will

To drive home

With me

Contemplating cigar smoke

Big fish and a piece of ass.

The corner vernacular
Rolls with the dice
Under lights
The shadow of hope
In the pot
Newspaper money
Spent on pavement competition
Skipping empty pockets
Home to hunger pains
And bread crumbs
Praying for tomorrow
More of the same
Let down
Comes my way
A better deal than most.

The paneling bar
Served a view out
A glass door
Women dangled
On the deck
Of an above ground
Pool water giggles
Wet panty delight
Highballs ice jiggles
Mammary awakenings
Glance at yourself
In the sliding glass door
I see through your tease
To a dream of relieving
Each other drawn
Away by guilt.

The wind up

In each other's lap

Some of our parents

Anger shot each other

Alive to realize

Maybe we are

Doing better

Than anyone realizes

We live in a lot of defenses

Let down this moment

Turns back time

We turn to each other

And make up

Our minds to support

The family

We chose to make It.

Art Brut

The colors of children
Smear to indeterminable
Flavors of emotion
q-tipped on cardboard
ripped from a box
fingerprint signed
the art of free-flow
between parent and child
a gallery of our complete
and honest selves.

In the principal
Moment she brush
Stroked my figure
Away to a new
Dream the colors differently
No model for this high
Art piece is not for sale
Attributed to many
But really from the creativity
Of one little one.

The offer comes

From outlines

In pencil

Erased with color

Camouflaged to viewers

The creators whisper

Behind funky framed lenses

That it all

Was supposed to be

Completely quite different

This showing affront

To the mystique of the painter.

Laughter is defined
Paint smeared every
Color in the rainbow
Gushes off canvas

Eye's Leak

Eyes leak words
Abundantly wet
And hysterical
Fast and slow
Reads on emotion
Stops and starts
Our ears numb
From the repeat
Of pain and confusion.

Candid reflections

Getting stoned

On marble

We repent luxury

And constantly piss

Regret is somber deterioration

Of the body and mind.

Back to the caliber

Of my past

Rediscovered in the pitfalls

Of life reasons us

To fringe points

Skydiving back

Into the lives of others

Faces in the Leaves

The decay of green
Cannot hide the pleasure
Of leaves falling
Around the silhouette
Of a brown stare
Into the sky
Capturing a child's
Dreams for the unknown
A shutterbug dad
Captures with a click

Hands too small

Squeezing for adventure

The shriek of excitement

Snows over life and death

Alike no other flake

Melts to the same thirst

Different states

Constantly are we falling

From one space

Landing another season

Without repeats

An audience kept

Growing different

Channels of our energy

Lost and rekindle

In swift passing

Our life is but

A child's fall dream

Partly true

Partly false.

The chieftains of backyard wilderness

Derive boundaries

Of falsely huge areas

Twisting in the wind

Chasing each other breathless

Growing up

The sounds of free spirits

Leaving room for life

Compromises the wishes

A young girl's laughter

Opens the song.

Powder sugar covered roofs

Of overflowing frosting

Little cake houses

Try standing as tall as midgets

Next to mother nature's winter

Sneeze of white ingredients

Ants in frozen sand

We are like

Laboring our lives

Back to normal

Buffalo moonshine and shoveling heart attacks.

Icicles start to go away
And then come back
Thinner in the legs
Not holding water
The gutter's spine
Is tired of the protrusion

Fish Food for Gumby

Keystone Hill

Cantor us beats
Coming from butterscotch candy
Snow falls on my tongue
A sleigh ride cautions
The horn of a car
On keystone the cobble
Jars steel blades
Smooth downhill
We hold on
For the concrete wall
Crash balls
On the boards
Of winters bumps.

The Viaduct

A television shouldered
On the foothill of tracks
Work boots slip
And regain the passage
To an iron shelf
Pushed from above
Laughing at the screeching
Halt of traffic
Doat Street shut down
By a TV
Under the viaduct
Panic echoes.

The Sacristy

This early
Church even empty of God
Planning the mischief
Of miss wrung bells
And kneeling too long
Delayed responses
To raised hands in judgment
Guilty eyes uncovered by laughter
Reprimands behind altars
Collars are added and removed
Like the kind harshness of the priest.

PAL

Super stadiums were in
The basements of Baptist
Church bowling alleys
Basketball courts
Trampled by chucks
And Keds
We honed our skills
For the pavement fields
Of east side paradise
The cheers haunt
The broken glass
A conch shell of old cheers
And the bickering intensity
Of adolescent men.

Pack 33

It wasn't the wholesome
Embodiment of the Eagle's rank
But reformed bullies and bad asses
Triumphantly labeled
Platoon leaders and scribes
Merit badges the opposition
of our environment
we drew praises for flags
and church hall presence
sashes of mother's sewing
three fingers to honor
Joe Skarpinski's command
Community service
For future misdeeds.

The Omega

Midnight blue
A boat on the rooftop
Of an eight track concert
Blue oyster cult
Hitchhikes on the skyway
Winds try to prematurely
Launch the skiff
We hold on laughing
To Godzilla god
The bronze backs
Off the break wall
Shoulders lured by
Mister twister
Green and yellow
The water erupted
Last sip of fish tales
In a miller can.

Frank's

Theodore and Block
Another round
Loretta asleep
On a stool
We reminisce
And predict
The future
Perils of alcohol
Parents rot away
From their kids
The alcoholic gene
Passes on buying rounds
The conservation of money
Exchanged for unconsciousness
Stumbling away from reality
Ending up cold and dehydrated
On the cemetery floor
We watch others
Taking our places
To spend themselves
Dead.

Schiller Park

The glass outfield
Covered by midget
White boys in droopy
Socks covered in diamond
Dust ourselves off up Doat
We bake ourselves parched
And stagger into the alley
To drink over filling
From the garden hose
A relief from the slavery
Of summer baseball
We were forbade to quit.

The White Sisters

Inside a fortress
To the solitude
Of feminism veiled
To God they cry
The sexuality to stop
Kneeling for selfish reasons
I came to understand
The true meaning of belief
In the chants of nuns
I couldn't see
All the pews were empty
Except for the face of me
Pondering the imprint
Of my kneel.

Indian Joe Witkowski

Through a window
He scouted me
Escaping tackles
On the blacktop
Under the lights
Highlighting speed
blinding
The defenses two hands
Untouched I score
The jersey number 30
Play for him now
Formally he says
East Buffalo Vikings.

The Moose

The moose fished
Seneca Lake
Camouflaging my voodoo
Jet crashed from the porch
Landing in the street
A tire abruptly
Crumples the plastic
My allowance invested
In the military air
Support is downed
Good old rocks
Ground ware fare
Retaliation that
Big bastard
No bleeds
From the head.

Crables

A shotgun blast
To the ice cream cooler
Mister Crable hated
Coming around
To the candy counter
Exposed from
Fortresses of inefficient
Appliances like mountains
For cover from robbery
He was forever frightened
Out of selling more penny
Candy counter from the misses
She would sneak me
Extra grape fish
For the two blocks
Home made me hungry
For sugar fixes.

Queeno

Brown plaid patterned
Assembled on blacktop
Schoolyard romances
Blossoming veils
Nuns flirting with reverends
In clown noses
Giggling diversion
Of sexual overtures
We line up
Before it gets too hot
We return to the classroom
Distracted by whispers
Outside the window.
And from the girl
Next to us.

Master's

Passing by the fire station
Kid what you got
A master's triple black raspberry
Broasted chicken
The men in uniform munch pizza
On a lazy summer night
The cone melts and
So does the firemen's time
Of safety hook and ladder
Nineteen minutes to anywhere
On the east side
I can still see
The spinning hands
Of the doe
White t-shirts and pants
All sauced up
Red but not too serious
Like a fire truck
To burning destruction.

Early flirtation

Up doat hill
Raced glica
Let her get ahead
Of me
The future
Mother of my daughter.

Behind Babiarz

Fort of railroad ties
To Wallace's for cans
Of twelve ounces
Covered in tree branches
Three feet deep
We pick out intruders
Hundreds of yards away
Another group of kids
Build their own
Hideaway
To sip some beers.

8 foot hoop

Intense games
On an eight foot hoop
A monster rejects
The trickery of midgets
Forced to dunk
Jump twice their height
To slap happy hands
Down through the clouds
Jammed the rim home.

Geist's Hardware

When portly suspenders
Wander summer flannel
Liniment waffling past bubblegum
Smells old in the tackle section
Plenty of lead
Sinkers and eagle claws
A daredevil spoon
Jointed rappala
The screen fixed
And a can of spray paint
For the rusty two speed
In the shed
Little engineers
Perfect the commerce
Of red second hand bicycles
A patch kit
On a racing slick
Back to skidding.

Barney's

In a meat freezer
White aprons
The screech of ban saws
Cutting bone down
T-bones and whole milk
pretzel sticks for the kids
sherbet push-ups and lime popsicles
prime candy and fresh meat
the school girls plaid
gathers on the steps
to exchange notes and kisses.

Lady Wallace

She was crowned
Mrs. Wallace how much
For last year's Easter candy
School kids asked the tease
With a full store
Haberly requests a slice
Of cheese distracts
The old man
Eight cents
For the chance
To reach for mouthfuls
Candy and cola
Guzzled profusely
The kid needs

Norm the barber

Could give you
A Poncherello
Feathered back
Style of mousse
Six bucks to a movie star

Herby the Cop

Badge to me
330
Special patrolman
Buffalo city
Beat my own driveway
Walkie talkie emergency calls
The cap gun drawn
Blue hat over the eyes
A nightstick drags behind
Like pants too big
The real guys
Just pull away laughing
If the kid only knew
What it's like
To be a cop.

Broadway Market

Hustling glances at the powdered bowties
Girl in a babushka
Blonde and real stock
Paper wrapping around fresh
Sausage the garlic permeates
The noses of chocolate bunnies
Hard boiled eggs camouflaged
In a rainbow of dye splashes
Pussy willows and water
Past history glides by
In the faces of vegetable
Truck drivers delivering
Memories of great grandma's
Past slaughtered butter lambs
Fresh rye and mustard
It is a happy time
To be Polish.

Rose Garden

A thousand yards in the rose garden
Gained at the expense of druggies
In cleats zig- zagging past elbows
Joints puffed
Out of skin
And jerseys
We slipped number thirty
And a tear away
To the light post
We spike another
Muddy victory
On schiller
Careers were made
At neighborhood
Spots like Frank's
We chipped bottles
Celebrating what
We knew as limited
Time.

Forman Street

Wiffle ball blues
On wereski field
A spaniel steals
The white toy in green
Grass wipes the saliva
Resume with spit balls
And foul outs
Even the dogs
Cheated on the east side
Summer afternoon
Too competitive
To feel hungry.

Fall Fight

Your yard
Crab apple
Swap in the back
Of the head
Two fences down
Colossi fires again
Moist green
Followed by the thud
A hard one
In the face
He giggles
Enraged rocks
Are the return
Fire.

East Side Tour circa 1980

This buffalo of mine
Full of thieves and whores
Dog beaters and cheaters
The lower middle class
Working stiff
Drunk from the night before
He literally bet the house
On where a fly would land
On some streets it still happens
Today the same lame truths
Of can't get out
With the white trash
Until next garbage day
Goes by and the pile up
Continues the saga
Of the slum.

Camaro spins

Out on Niagara ice
Falls frozen winter
Night degrees 360
Screams belt out
Snow banks stopping
The cascade of youth
Endangered by the wheel
Of a seductive woman
Hits the gas again
Straight away like
Nothing happened
Near death
Back over the bridge.

Twin action

Charlie sold
Canadians and kohos
Orange balls
And thick tape
Protecting blades
On blacktop
Hobby shop paint
Adorning goalie masks
The foam from appliances
Shoe laced around knees
And ankles padded
Thud of snap shots
Whistle through
Windows on a convent
Shatter the nun
Gives chase
To the whole
Fifth grade.

Keystone fields

Around the corner
Bad kids lived
They blocked
The route to
The next street
Fraught with unsavory
Carl's and the like
Wrecking kids new bikes
The winter gloves off
Punches exchanged
For wrong glances
Get you black eyed.

Milk Machine

We knocked it over
But depended on it
Like mother's for quarters
For quarts of guzzling
The jarring ten block sprint
The best thing about a corner
Used to be the milk machine.
And the kids that drank
From it.

Aunt Ann

In an upper flat
Across the street
Three generations
Under a roof
Of a steel workers
Father who kept
Golf course green lawns
Spaghetti was served
Piping hot with birch beer
And interrogation about
My home life
Is another story.

Polish Mass

Monsignor Gabalski
Hands raised towards
Queen of Peace
Ten thirty confusion
Interpreting the sign
Of the cross
Standing and kneeling
Un-uniformly confused
By syllables of consonants
Praying to survive
Embarrassment of not knowing
My own peoples language.

The Substance of Poverty

Reckless streets abandoned cars

Boarded up taverns

Junkies in the cold

Space between surviving

And dying in the streets

East buffalo roams

The side

Groups in the hoods

And camps of whities

Old poles too stubborn

To leave it to fate

Urban America is crying

In the pain of power

Concentrating on too much

To remember being a little bit hungry

And a little bit broke

These streets are too lonely

For hope doesn't come

In windowless homes.

I aim to see

You've got no choice

Walking the streets

Numbing the pain of John's

Terrified Maturity

Terrified Maturity-

Terrified in the small
Spaces of time
Reflect corners
Condemned to moments
Of grammar school
Become middle age
Face away from the class
All waiting to hear
What you have to say
After all this time
Searching genesis and the cow
Sunjaya and me
Fall asleep with
No better understanding
But an agreement to keep
Trying to find each other
In violence and chaos
We defend our peace.

The door to success

Opened and so what

To happiness you apologize

For the rainstorm

You brought in your comfort

To the sanctity of heirs

Put on by those who think talent

Relieves you to think

Responsibly about

The time we have

Should never have taken

For granted

the great gift

Of more minutes

So about this money

So concerned about

Secret incomes

Begged to buy

The corporations scream

You need

To give me your money

Trigger Man and the Pussycats

Loaded I stumble
Past guns and fishnets
Around ankles
Contorted and bent
Boots the only skin
Left to imagination
All this desire mine
Behold that new aura
Of moist healing
The daily grind cured
By stripped friction
Of enough anonymity
To let yourself go
Without fear
You rush to tremble
Quiver and exclaim
Freedom on six inches
And the head of a mallet.

Virtuous

P

O

S

T

U

Re excite me

About being bad

Uncross your legs

Show me

Your special little spot

Conservative but panty less.

The sheets are a starch white canvas

A shroud of our entanglement

Evidence of revolutions

Top and bottom

Behind

Breathlessly clinging

I can see your nipples

Engulfed in the wrinkled canvas

Living art

In a white sheet

Entangled with me

My finger stroking your back.

Penis Monologue

This sucks

Oh please yes

This constant throbbing

An affliction

Need you

To take this from me

Soothe me in warm

Vaginal humidity

All day stuck inside

I like that kind of punishment.

Lovejoy girl

Here is my

Offering

A roll in the grass

A joint

My breasts

The rest on Friday

At my babysitting job

It will be like we live

This together thing

A little fast

Pussy is all I'm looking for

Ward off the dogs

Isn't I like you

Enough

For a girl from lovejoy

You do that well

Kept the grass stains

On for days we talked about

A roll in the grass

And me never showing up

To your babysitting job.

Whiskey rain

Felt freedom
In the music
The swagger
The high of it
All calling me
The steamy breath
Of manhole covers
Saxophone streets
Drunken laughs
Stocking feet in puddles
Vagina temptations
From the rear
Pulling up
Pants quickly
Discarded
The fence you
Momentarily climb
Without leaving
The ground
I thrust you
Above
Me pleasure humid

And verbal

You can hear

The in out

Echoed under

The bleachers

You finally let

Go

Taken by pleasure

The public is oblivious

To the smiles

From your zipper.

I ripen outside

My peel

The meat

Snakes through

Cotton openings

It anticipates

Your lips

My eyes watch

Your juicy behind

The silk

The prize is open

For the business

Of my fingers

You lick

And suck

Me into submission

You jiggle and whine.

The pole stops
Legs slither
To the floor
A spread
For dollars
Getting fantasy
For tuition
The humor goes
Like track marks
To nowhere
In back rooms
Giving it all
The trigger man
Tug leaves
A stain
On the carpet
Everyone's DNA.

Buttons undone
Reveal the life line
Of nipples and breasts
Seemingly sad
To see anyone
Begins the joyful
Tug and test
The juices flow
From a faux feeding frenzy
No nourishment
Just selfish indulgence
Respiration jiggles
Flushed faces
Relax in
The afterglow of sex.

Pulsating boxers

Strive outside the boundaries

Of cotton

Your hands approach

Extending you reach

For control

Talking your way through

Lubrication

Pulling and pushing

Tugging and groping

In the dark

You crawl on your knees

Until a release

Comes just what you asked for

Still pumping empty

To the glow of your breasts.

The Weeping Wall of Graffiti

Somewhere in the cracks
Of alley walls
Paint runs off words
A communication of savagery
And despair spray painted
The impoverished tears
Of hunger and violence
Pain in the design
A calling out
White folks put on your brakes
We're suffering
Like third world soldiers
In a war on ourselves

Stares call out

discomfort sized up

Through a rear view mirror

A hand sign

To let you know

See ya bitch

In my neighborhood

All we got

Is pride

Rolling through the stop sign

Marty's Grille rescues

With Budweiser

And Polish-English

Over rapping base

Inside like thirty-five

Years ago my Uncles

Sat in stools hard-hat

Back in time

Steel plant paychecks

Ruled the east side

Letter carrier
The bricks held together
By masonry of confessions
In code or outright
They talk to those who
Listen about crimes of quality
Of life mine's suffering
At the hands of suppression
These streets talk to the walls
The walls whisper hate
In the blood of my brother
Is spilled constantly
And you're worried
About paint.

www.ingramcontent.com/pod-product-compliance
Lightning Source LLC
Chambersburg PA
CBHW022026090426
42739CB00006BA/300